SIMPLY SCIENCE

The Simple Science of

MATTER

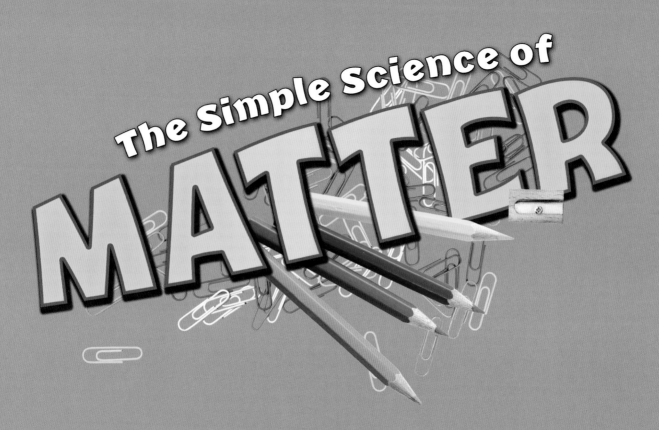

Emily James

raintree

a Capstone company — publishers for children

Raintree is an imprint of Capstone Global Library Limited, a company incorporated in England and Wales having its registered office at 264 Banbury Road, Oxford, OX2 7DY – Registered company number: 6695582

www.raintree.co.uk
myorders@raintree.co.uk

Edited by Jaclyn Jaycox
Designed by Jenny Bergstrom
Original illustrations © Capstone Global Library Limited 2018
Picture research by Jo Miller
Production by Tori Abraham
Originated by Capstone Global Library Limited
Printed and bound in China

ISBN 978 1 4747 4348 8
21 20 19 18 17
10 9 8 7 6 5 4 3 2 1

British Library Cataloguing in Publication Data
A full catalogue record for this book is available from the British Library.

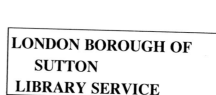
Acknowledgements
We would like to thank the following for permission to reproduce photographs:
Shutterstock: 123dartist, 18-19, Africa Studio, back cover (top), 10 (right), AllaSaa, 13, Aryut Tantisoontornchai, 14, Blend Images, 22, Dragon Images, 6, fotomirk, 29 (left), George Dolgikh, 11, Grandpa, 23, jakkapan, 28, JeniFoto, front cover, Lesterman, 25, MicroOne, 20-21, MNStudio, 26-27, Nadja Gellermann, 8-9, Petr Malyshev, 24, Photographee.eu, 4-5, phugunfire, 29 (inset), Pingpao, 12, Sebastian Duda, 10-11 (background), sebra, back cover, Sergey Novikov, 15, Suthichai Hantrakul, 5 (inset), Tom Wang, 17, trekandshoot, 9 (inset), unguryanu, 16, Valentin Valkov, 7, 10 (left). Design elements: Shutterstock: Cameramannz, Rose Carson

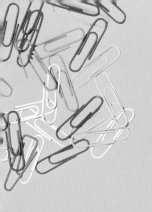

CONTENTS

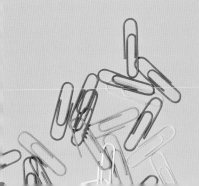

What in the world is matter?

It's a bird! It's a plane! It's MATTER!
Matter is all around you. If you can see,
touch, smell or taste something, it's matter.

Your toys, bed and house
are matter. So are stars! Matter
is anything that takes up space
and has mass.

Air is matter too. You may not see air, but it takes up space. Think about blowing up a balloon. The air you blow in takes up space. It makes the balloon bigger and bigger!

Some things have more matter than others. A car has more matter than a bicycle. It's bigger and heavier.

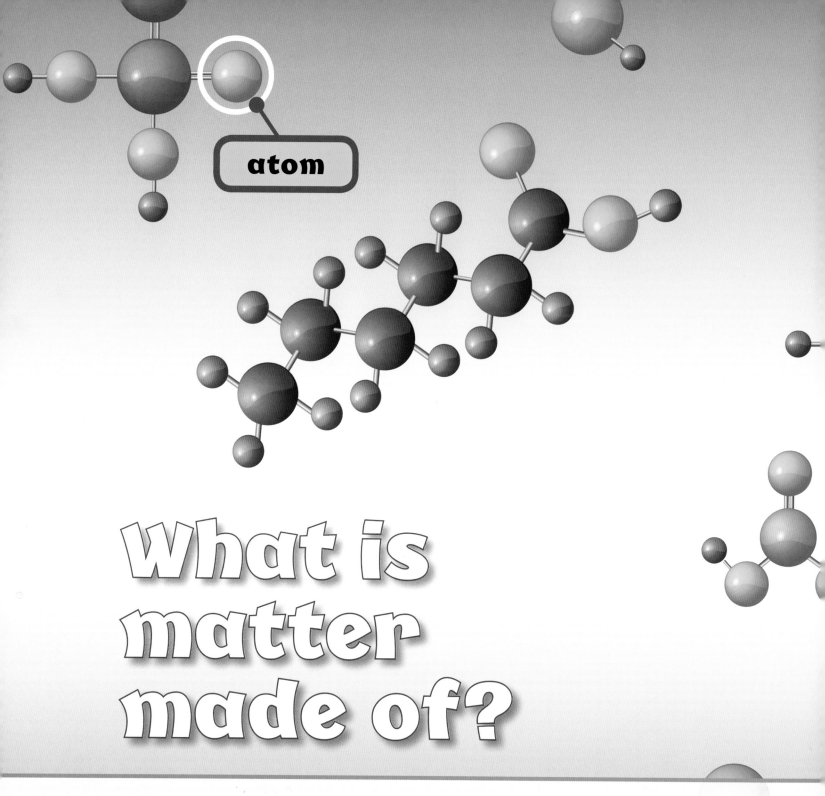

atom

what is matter made of?

Matter is made of tiny particles called atoms. They are too small to see. Think of atoms as building blocks. When atoms join together, they make molecules.

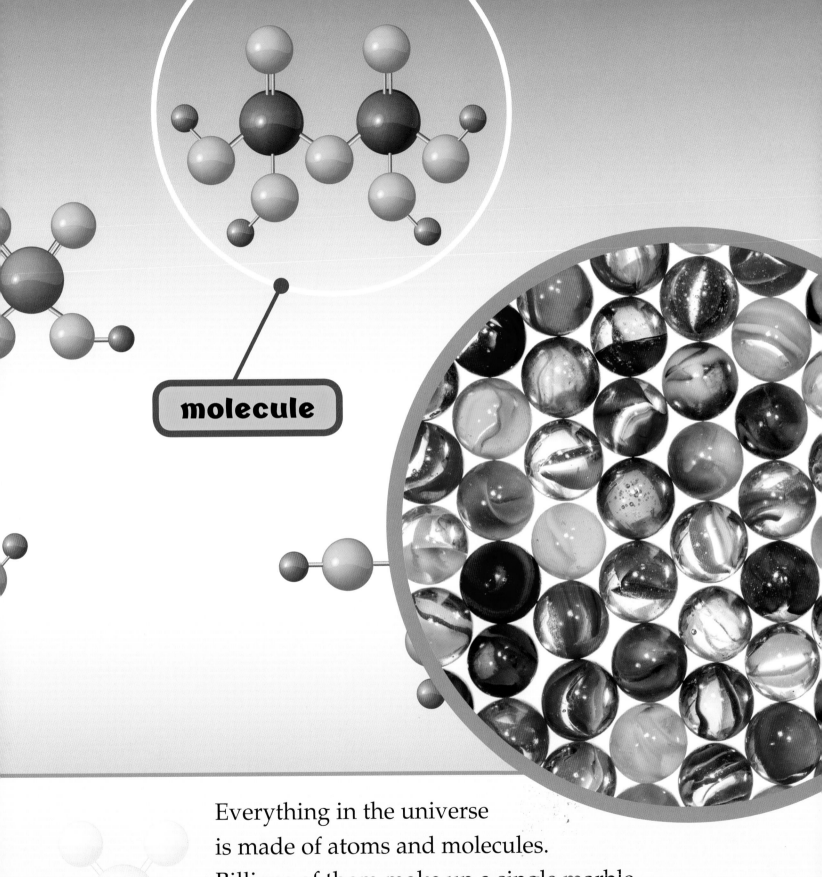

molecule

Everything in the universe
is made of atoms and molecules.
Billions of them make up a single marble.

solid

liquid

States of matter

Matter comes in three main forms, or states.
It can be a solid, liquid or gas.

gas

Each state has properties. A property describes matter. Colour, smell and feel are properties of matter.

A solid has shape. You can hold it.
Solids can be bouncy or stretchy.
They can feel hard, soft or squishy.

You can change the shape of a solid. You can break a pencil in half. You can bend a paper clip. You can squeeze clay.

A liquid does not have its own shape. You can pour it, splash in it or spill it.

A liquid takes the shape of whatever is holding it. Juice takes the shape of the bottle it's in. If you spill the juice, it spreads out into a puddle.

A gas does not have a shape. You cannot hold it or pour it. A gas floats anywhere it can. When put in a container, it spreads out to fill the space.

The air all around you is gas. Most gases can't be seen, but you can sometimes feel them. Wind is air molecules bumping into you!

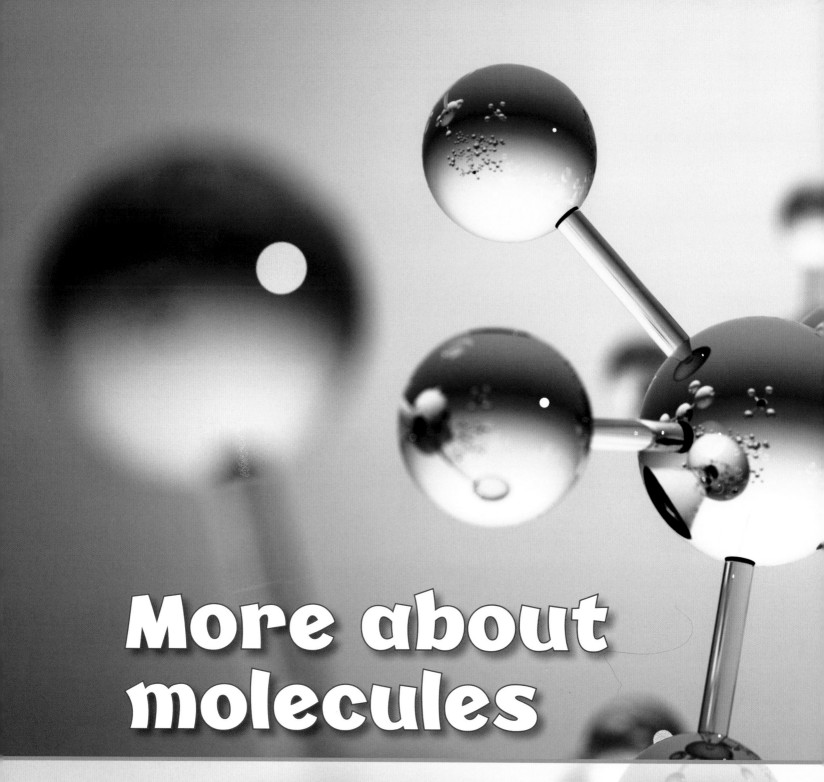

More about molecules

Molecules are always moving.
Gas, liquid and solid molecules
move in different ways.

Gas molecules are spread far apart.
They move around really fast! They
zing in many directions to fill the space.

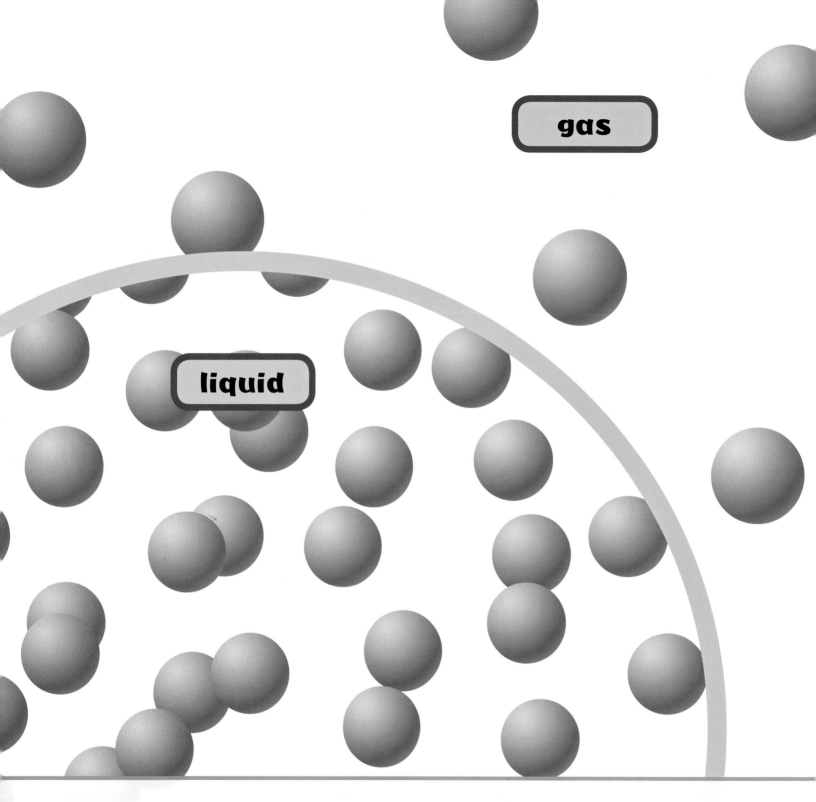

gas

liquid

Liquid molecules are closer together. They also
move around a lot, but they move more slowly.
They bump into each other and stick together.
That movement is what makes liquids flow.

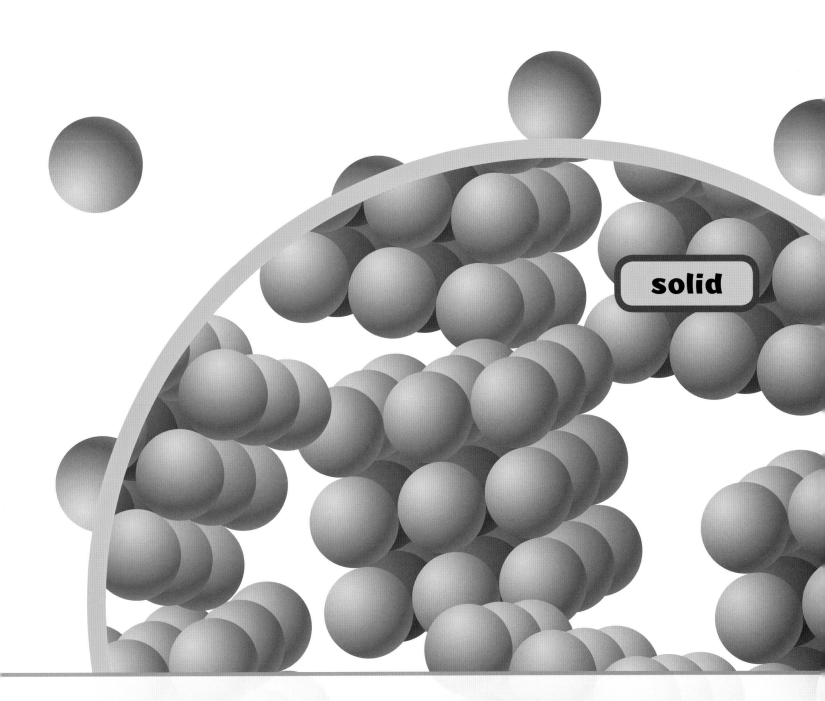

solid

Solid molecules are packed tightly
together. They move, but they don't
move very fast or far. It's hard for solid
molecules to move past each other.

Changing states

Some matter can change from a solid to a liquid. This change is called melting. When some solids become hot, they melt. Ice cream melts outside on a hot day. It turns into liquid.

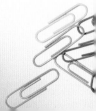

A liquid can turn into a solid too.
When water freezes, it turns into ice.

Some liquids can also turn into a gas. This change happens when the liquid is very hot. Hot water turns into a gas called steam. Steam puffs out of a kettle when the water boils.

Gases turn into liquids when they get cold.
When you take the lid off a hot saucepan,
it's covered with water. Why? The steam
cooled and turned back into water.

Matter is everywhere

Look around you. What do you see?
Take a deep breath. What do you smell?

What do you feel under your feet?
Matter! Isn't it wonderful?

Blow it up!

A gas expands to fill the space of the container that holds it. Try this experiment to see how expanding gas can inflate a balloon.

What you need:

a funnel

3 teaspoons (15 ml)
  of bicarbonate of soda

a balloon

2 tablespoons (30 ml)
  of white vinegar

a plastic water bottle

What you do:

- Use a funnel to pour bicarbonate of soda into the balloon. Set aside.
- Pour vinegar into the plastic bottle.
- Pinch the neck of the balloon. Holding the balloon upside down, stretch the opening of the balloon over the neck of the bottle. Do not let the bicarbonate of soda fall into the bottle yet.
- When the balloon is on the neck of the bottle, un-pinch the balloon. Shake the balloon so all of the bicarbonate of soda falls into the bottle. Watch what happens to the balloon.

- Bicarbonate of soda and vinegar have a chemical reaction when mixed. They give off gas. The molecules in the gas expand and inflate the balloon.

GLOSSARY

boil heat water or another liquid until it bubbles;
water boils when it reaches 100 degrees Celsius
(212 degrees Fahrenheit)

container object, such as a box or jar, that is used to
hold something

liquid matter that is wet and can be poured, such as water

mass amount of material in an object

molecule atoms making up the smallest unit of
a substance

particle tiny piece of something

property quality of a material, such as colour, hardness
or shape

solid substance that holds its shape

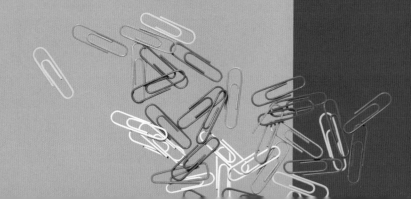

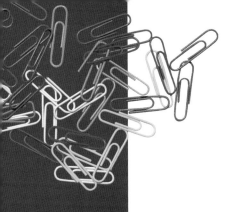

FIND OUT MORE

BOOKS

Matter (Moving Up With Science), Peter Riley (Franklin Watts, 2016)

States of Matter (Physical Science), Abbie Dunne (Raintree, 2017)

States of Matter (Science in a Flash), Georgia Amson-Bradshaw (Franklin Watts, 2017)

WEBSITES

www.bbc.co.uk/education/topics/zkgg87h
This website includes more information about solids, liquids and gases.

www.dkfindout.com/uk/science/solids-liquids-and-gases
Find out more about solids, liquids and gases.

COMPREHENSION QUESTIONS

1. Everything in the world is made up of atoms and molecules. What are molecules? Hint: Use the glossary for help!
2. Matter comes in three forms, or states. What are they?
3. Some matter can change states. Can you think of a solid that can turn into a liquid?

INDEX

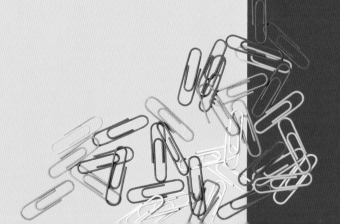